# The Frozen Continent:
# Antarctica

by Laura Crawford

**Scott Foresman**
is an imprint of

Glenview, Illinois • Boston, Massachusetts • Mesa, Arizona
Shoreview, Minnesota • Upper Saddle River, New Jersey

**Photographs**

Every effort has been made to secure permission and provide appropriate credit for photographic material. The publisher deeply regrets any omission and pledges to correct errors called to its attention in subsequent editions.

Unless otherwise acknowledged, all photographs are the property of Pearson Education, Inc.

Photo locators denoted as follows: Top (T), Center (C), Bottom (B), Left (L), Right (R), Background (Bkgd)

**Cover** Corbis; **1** DK Images; **3** DK Images; **4** (TL, C) Corbis; **5** DK Images; **6** (B) Corbis, (CL) Getty Images; **7** (CR) DK Images, (T) NASA; **8** (T) Corbis, (CL) National Weather Service (NWS) Collection/NOAA; **9** (C) Digital Wisdom, Inc., (B) Getty Images; **10** (C, B) Corbis; **12** Corbis.

ISBN 13: 978-0-328-39418-0
ISBN 10:    0-328-39418-1

Antarctica is the coldest place on Earth. It is a frozen continent covered in ice. The South Pole is on Antarctica. The South Pole is the farthest south that you can go!

Antarctica

Antarctica is very windy. It is also very dry. Antarctica is so dry that scientists call it a desert. The small amount of snow that falls there never melts. It is moved around by the wind until it freezes into ice.

Orca whales

Leopard seal

Few people other than scientists have been to Antarctica. It costs a lot of money to send food and supplies there. But penguins, seals, fish, and whales live there year-round.

Emperor penguin

Scientists study the weather in Antarctica. They use a radio called an acoustic sounder. It sends beeping sounds high up into the air. The beeping sounds make an echo that tells scientists the wind's speed and direction.

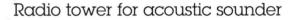

Radio tower for acoustic sounder

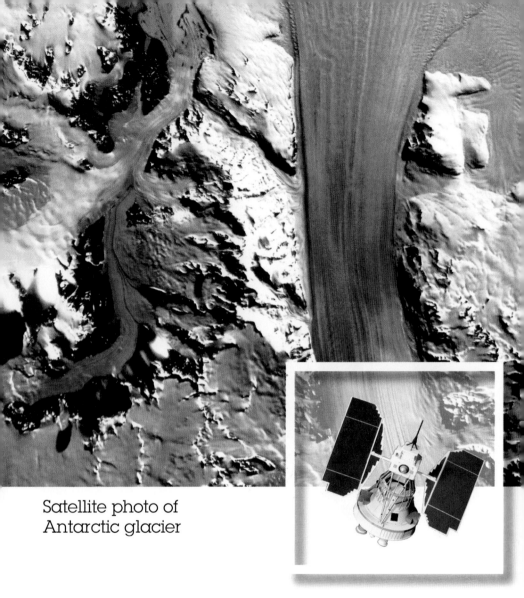

Satellite photo of
Antarctic glacier

Satellites help scientists study
the weather in Antarctica. Weather
information from the satellites is sent
down to Earth.

Antarctic weather balloon
and research station

Scientists in Antarctica also study the
weather with balloons. Each day, they
launch the balloons into the air. Radios
attached to the balloons record information
about the air.

Scientists are learning about global warming on Antarctica. Global warming happens when air pollution traps heat inside the Earth's atmosphere. Some parts of Antarctica have become warmer. Other parts are growing colder.

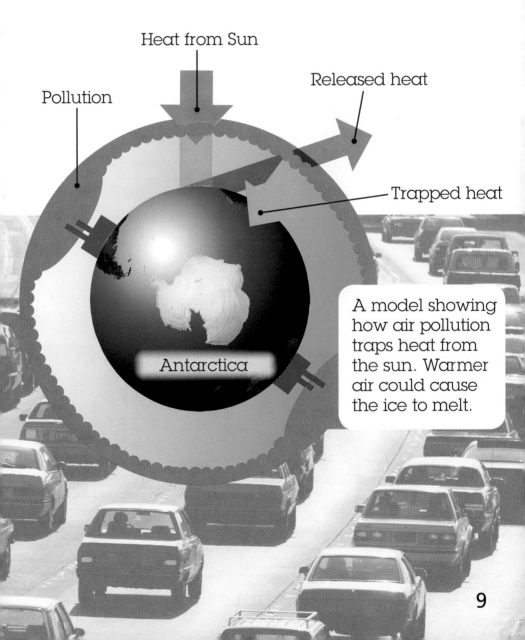

Heat from Sun

Released heat

Pollution

Trapped heat

Antarctica

A model showing how air pollution traps heat from the sun. Warmer air could cause the ice to melt.

Emperor penguins spend their whole lives in Antarctica. Penguins cannot fly. But they are very good swimmers. They use their feet and flippers to swim. Penguins use their bills to preen, or clean and smooth their feathers.

Bill

Flipper

Feet

Female emperor penguins lay one egg. The male emperor penguin takes care of the egg. He snuggles and cuddles the egg with his feet. Soon the chick is ready to hatch. It pecks at the shell until it breaks.

For emperor penguins, seals, fish, and whales, the climate in Antarctica is just right. Scientists will continue to study Antarctica's climate and watch for signs of change. In this way they are protecting the animals that make their home there.